El Duende

Marlene A. Fulcher

A catalogue record for this book is available from the National Library of Australia

Copyright © 2020 Marlene Fulcher

All rights reserved.

ISBN-13: 978-1-922343-23-9

Linellen Press
265 Boomerang Road
Oldbury, Western Australia
www.linellenpress.com.au

Dedication

This compilation of poetry is dedicated to my wonderful family, members, past and present, of The Society of Women Writers WA and Karrinyup Writers' Club Inc., who gave workshops on some of the forms in this collection and who encouraged my steps as a writer, and to Helen Iles who made this publication possible.

Marlene A Fulcher

According to Wikipedia - El duende is the spirit of evocation. It comes from inside as a physical/emotional response to art. It is what gives you chills, makes you smile or cry as a bodily reaction to an artistic performance that is particularly expressive.

Contents

Dedication iii
Contents v
A Celebration of Friendship 1
A Gift from Gran 2
a shadow lingers 4
A Touch of Sunlight 6
Always Tomorrow 8
Another Time, Another You 9
At the End of the Line 10
Auschwitz 11
Axiom 12
Between the Lines 13
Between the Spaces 14
Beyond the Covenant 15
Beyond the Frame 16
Birth of a Poet 17
Can I Tell You Once Again 18
Can't Stop the Music 19
City Nights 20
Clear is the Night 21
Confessional 22
Creativity 23

Cross Winds	24
Day on the Rocks	25
Death…	26
Down the Line	27
Do you remember	28
El Duende	29
Enchantress of the Forest	30
Equestrian	31
Firelight Shadows	32
first step only one step away	33
For my Mother - Dulcie Jane	34
Ghost Gum	35
I Never Knew	36
Illusive Shadow	37
In Memoriam	38
In Memory of a Friend	39
In the Rhythm of Rain	40
Interlude	41
In the Stillness	42
Inner Child	44
Last Call	45
Legacy of Love	46
Liquid Shadows	49
Living Drums	50
Made to Measure	51
Magic Of The Night	53

May Day for Australia	54
Moonspell	55
Nightmares	56
On Mount Parnassus	57
Overture to Night	58
Paint the Wind	59
Painted Devils	60
Paradise	61
Portals	62
Portrait of a Tree	63
Recall	64
Rhubarb and Plums	65
Riding the Wind	67
Sanctuary - My Hearts Crystal Cave	68
Scarred	71
Sea Sprite	72
Sestina of a Letter Home - 1917	73
Setting The Stage	75
Smouldering Embers	76
Soft Voice, Rich and Clear	78
Somewhere in France	81
Song of Twilight	84
Tabula Rasa	85
Through the Darkness	86
Through the Mist	87
To the Tree Outside my Window	88

To Your Dear Self	89
Trust	91
Twilight of the Gods	92
Undiminished Symphony	94
Watching Snails	95
When rain mists the blue	96
Why?	98
Writer on the Bus	99
Yesterday and Today	100

A Celebration of Friendship

There is a time, a time for giving birth,
For living free, believing all the words,
The musical enchantment of their worth
When whispered in a garden full of birds;
Recalling youth, a promise made with love:
A time to smile, to hug a new born child,
To make new friends and thank the Lord above
For life's contentment's, just a touch of wild.
But now it's time, my friend, to celebrate.
For thanking you who taught me how to seize
The moment, hold to hope, appreciate
And share the little things - a song to ease
The pain, bring colour to a memory;
To hear life's music, live in harmony.

A Gift from Gran

Miranda's doll is all brand new
she got it Christmas day
my little doll was made by Gran
all soft for hugs and play

Miranda's doll needs batteries
to walk and talk and sing
my little doll needs only love
to do most anything

Miranda's doll can take a walk
but then it has to stop
my little doll can walk and walk
until we both do drop

Miranda's doll can really say
some clever words I know
my little doll says only things
to set the heart a glow

With my dear doll, my little Ann
my world is always bright
we talk and share our special thought
our dreams and bed at night

Miranda says she loves her doll
and often takes her out
but when I see my little Ann
I know what love's about

a shadow lingers

Centre ring, you bow, juggle
red, yellow, green – an act
or a walk in the sun.
Behind a painted smile you dance
stumble into a somersault
dust off.
You rush forward bucket high
toss paper streamers
We dodge, laugh.

    Your attention stays
    With the small boy by my side
    Bandanna now, no ginger curls
        Smile, clown, smile
        In your eyes…

You pull forever-hanky
from your pocket
wipe away a tear, turn
climb the ladder.
Your clown shoes
no longer fit the spaces
Rope tightens, you venture one foot
sway, slip, regain balance
each move rehearsed.

You glance once more
in our son's direction
his sallow face flushed with laughter.
    Smile clown, smile
      for in your eyes…

A Touch of Sunlight

Lord Gold' roses bloom.
I hadn't notice
their first blush -
Tawny Port leaves,
lemon petals bursting
free.

Where is that dark-haired girl -
curls bunched together
with bright satin bow -
the girl,
instant woolies packed away,
ran to the park,
swung higher and higher,
laughter echoing in leaves,
her face tilted to sun -
wanting – believing
she belonged.

I remember -
She Wore a Yellow Ribbon.
If every rose bush – tree,
wore a yellow ribbon,
would that dark-haired girl
return.

I walk inside,
place a single rose
in a slender vase -
a touch of sunlight

Always Tomorrow

Dark night whispers
every breath
wings of memory
seasons gone

Wind on water stirs
whirlpool of words
left unspoken
visions of regret

Mellow light   and
you forget the nightmares
promises made   to say
I love you — I care
to listen   — laugh
hug more than the trees

Another Time, Another You

Insistent shadows
another time.
A fancy dress ball
music, laughter
dancing, firecrackers
    Ten, nine eight, seven
    you smile, Mum and Dad
    move to your side
    six, five, four – enfold you,
    hug – three, two, one -
    they kiss each other,
    kiss you.

A leisurely stroll homewards
Grown-ups sing –
play cards, charades.
You play tag under stars -
giggle,
Friends gather
the honky-tonk pulsates
old time songs – no lullabies
You are eleven -
 almost grown up.
It's a Happy New Year!

At the End of the Line

She hears the child
in your voice
      talks fast
      of Cimmerian clouds
      rainbows after rain
heeds your sighs, listens
attends words before unspoken.

Auschwitz

The tour bus pulls to a halt.
Heavy with silence, we walk,
are not separated, women from the men,
ordered to strip, yet stand exposed,
frozen, in front of glass viewing rooms.

Tossed, atop one another,
victim's clothes, tailored, shop bought,
stitched by women around kitchen tables,
share the same fate.

Spectacles,
never seeing what was to come,
now bear witness.

Shoes, once worn by these souls
never again to feel soft grass, dance
to music of their homeland.

Zyklon B gas canisters piled high,
suffocate. I push one foot before the other.
Guide's voice, a whispered thread,
unable to drown shouts, screams,
 reverberating along the chamber walls,

    I wipe tears, free to walk through the gate.
    but the images remain

Axiom

She holds the moon in her hands
He sits
  watches stars sparkle, die
  She understands the fascination
  But cannot stay.

      There is too much truth
      In their dying.

Between the Lines

'Young Girl Missing'
Red light
Dark room Negative image
young girl swinging
'Police Make An Arrest'
White light Dark room Spot-lit questions
detained man snaps
'Suspect Charged'
Blue light ride
Dark room
Nightmare image lone man swinging

'Another Death In Custody'

Between the Spaces

War-shifting loyalties
homes lost, timeless treasures
left behind, never collected anew –
fine silver, great grandmother's
sturdy clay pot,
gilt edged frames, faces
smiling from within
eloquent in the retelling.

I trace yellowed pages
written – never shared
buttons left unstitched
holes never mended
linger, album on my lap
relive shaped memories
unfolding success
contemporary new life.

Images blur
I finger her smile, recall
the lilt of her voice, but
I never heard angels sing, for
upon a lonely hillside, where
emerald shamrocks grow
she left behind her sons.

Beyond the Covenant

We think and laugh everyday
hold keys to the gifts of night
hear music in wind, dream
of golden winged dragons
from the East, understand
beyond the promise of a new day
    When a fiery dragon
    flies in from the north
    will we behold blood and war
    or flames of transformation
    walk through, track
    the fragmented soul of peace
    release the snow-bound dragon
    to spread again her wings
        Or retrace our steps
        watch a golden sun
        set behind aqua wings
        think, laugh and cry?

Beyond the Frame

Your face beneath the glass.
I trace the frame – smile
You worried about not being here,
You are in my heart
The many gifts
In your words, stories, poems.
You shimmer
through the lives you touched
your smile floating at the edge
of a memory.
If only I could tell you –
But maybe,
you already know.

Birth of a Poet

Heart lies low
awaits new birth
those special words
that flow heaven to earth
unchain the mind
render forth verse
now only echoes
in the depth of my soul.

Can I Tell You Once Again

Uneasy sleep evokes a demon
nightmare of dying alone
let calm unseat the ghoulish icon
bring to mind what you've always known
I'd be here to see you through
to sing the song you love to hear
Have I Told You Lately That I Love you,
whisper sweet memories in your ear
of times we shared, held to our heart
You smile, high cheek bones defined
as you slip into a trance, depart –
leaving only love

Can't Stop the Music

Its syncopating music makes me move
And sway, that *Dancing Queen*, old ABBA beat
Still has me smiling, swinging to the groove.
Pulsating rhythm rushes to my feet.
My step is lighter, quicker than before
Each note so clear I'm taken to a time
I Could Have Danced all Night across the floor
Believed in shooting stars, and summertime.
The mood has changed and I'm remembering
Another past, a *String of Pearls*, my Mum –
The way she smiled, encouraged me to sing
Is stirring, beating like a distant drum.
My mother's treasured gift is mine to keep –
The love of music weaving clear and deep

City Nights

In a dark corner
a bundle of rags
hang
from an alcoholic frame
    In the street
    angry blades
    flash
    teenage boys
    struggle
    emptiness destroys
    swells into crime
        Under the lights
        footfalls and shadows
        hide the reality
        of city nights

Clear is the Night

Shackleton said – ambitions
become clearer in the dark –
I too love
the hours after sunset,
time of lavender dreams.
Asking the hard questions
listening to silence
each breath
every heartbeat
to hear answers
echo through the darkness

Confessional

Tormented dreams of passion,
Trapped
inside a stiff white collar,
fuelled from behind
black
veiled partitions.

    "Forgive me father
    for I have sinned."

She opens
like a full-blown flower,
 invites me in. I dare not.
The woman next door
parades
in nothing at all.
They cannot know
they are the torment
of my dreams.

    "I absolve you
    my daughters.
    Now go!

    Go in peace."

Creativity

Deep in my bones, I know you,
know you belong –
your name now only words
I no longer understand.

know you belong
but you have left
I no longer understand
can't hear you

You have left
your flow veiled
I can't hear you
thoughts, ideas dead

Your flow veiled
name now only words
faint images
but deep in my bones, I know you

Cross Winds

Whisper of places far away
hum a melody, reach deep inside
filter through
caress my face

In the air, exotic perfumes
desert sands, striped tents
girls veiled – eyes
sending invitation

Palm trees bow their heads
to visions of a rolling sea
transport me to a land
of rustling trees,
scented wood

I dance beneath
wind-tossed sky
cherish the magic
that allows me to see
the lay of many lands

Day on the Rocks

By wave-washed sands
he strolls
pristine shorts
Rolex   Reeboks
tackle box   gear
and sun-tanned companion

On water-carved rocks
he balances
proud   resolute
Casts a line   rewinds
launches again

Seagulls cry approval
as repeatedly
he plays the game
Exercise?
A fish for supper?

Or for
the long-legged lady
rapt in the pages
of her book

Death...

I perceive your darker nature well
have learnt this world is not judicious
chances are lost
opportunities come uninvited
you toss a coin
a mother and her child
taken
spin a wheel…

I acknowledge your macabre rituals
Rebel against the alternative
Never quite fathom my fear
of skeletons with scythes

Come as Thanatos
Son of night
Or as the grim reaper
Point your emaciated finger
Dance your dance
You are but a doorway
      A transformation

Down the Line

Come on young fella and give us a hand
the herd must be mustered I need every man
Over the ridges and onward we ride
to round up the cattle from plains far and wide
As shadows grow longer and day's work is done
it's back to the camp for father and son
We've gathered the cattle from gully and scrub
now challenge a plate of old 'Cookie's' grub
Dark dusty hills stand high in the night
backdrops to fires that burn warm and bright
men swapping stories of an arduous drive
intensity of heat, the flood they survive
Long before daylight has coloured the sky
with thundering hooves over red earth we fly
across swollen rivers and down mountain side
relying on horses specially bred for the ride
We did a month's work so now we can rest
then homeward we go and I ride with the best
across this vast land of dust and hot sun
back to the Homestead where clear waters run
Many a drive I have done since that day
and now to my son I can proudly say
Come on young fella give us a hand
the herd must be mustered, helicopter manned.

Do you remember

when you remembered longer
than a minute or two
when you never forgot why you
came into the kitchen
the bedroom, bathroom
puzzled when you
found an answer
forgot the question.
Were you coming or going
when you hesitated mid
passageway.
Can you name
the book you last read
you finished it yesterday, or
was it last week
latest movie, or
when you saw it?
Don't fret
 if you can't remember
it wasn't important, but if
perchance it was, don't worry
you won't remember
you forgot.

El Duende

Wind Goblin - Creative force

Like all lonely hungry things
he dances
flirts with shadows
stirs the desert earth
gathers power.
He carries stories, dreams
rides across air and sea
in the cry of gulls
ruffle of sails.
I have felt him move in solitude,
through music
a single word.

Enchantress of the Forest

Hair
ripples of Titian gold,
Her pale face dewy fresh,
high cheek bones clearly defined,
dark eyes wide,
searching the unknown.
Her smile uncertain of direction;
her wraith body dressed in black
and forest green.
Child of the woods
delicate,
untamed
A startled fawn quivering
impatient to be loved -
too frail to be held.
A faerie creature
caught
between sunlight and shadow.

Equestrian

Given freedom's reign
she rides well
her untamed stud
bridles
his every move
with fire and passion.
Yielded full command
she is master of the game
and
freedom reigns

Firelight Shadows

Hair
ribbons unfurling
reflect sunrise, sunset
petticoats flirt with flames
feet weave symbols in the earth
Gypsy violins
unravel a deeper knowing
as she whirls around
the camp fire

She had learnt the steps
danced the dance
bled without dying

Spent
she drops to one knee
before her dark-eyed lover
      The dance has ended
      The music plays on.

first step only one step away

To be or not to be
perchance to... die
we heard the Prince of Denmark cry
Perchance I say to continue living
lead a life both free and giving
erect a platform, take a stand
play a part in the big brass band
march to music of a different sway
    The first step – one step away.

For my Mother
Dulcie Jane

Lace curtains softly sighed as scented breezes blew
Our words were tremulous and few - we knew
that summer's last soft glow of gold would melt your will
and though you're gone, your presence lingers still

in memories that drift on music you once played
so sweetly, like a lover's serenade -
in every rainbow bubble, every sparkling stream.
You were my staff, my rod, my hope, my dream

You shared your gifts, inspired children, women, men
to love and value music, song - and then
to dance, to treasure life, to pray. Your loyalty
your quiet strength and true humility

now gives me hope, belief in God's reward, new life
for you, worthy daughter, mother, wife -
a life exempt of pain - so blessed with angels' song
And though you're gone, your presence lingers on

Ghost Gum

I sit thinking of you.
Through glass
a tree calls.
I open my window
feel the soft kiss
of evening.
Know
why leaves sparkle.

In night-time shadows
I fold my arms
around its trunk
nail file smooth
against my skin
hear it hum
with dream-time songs.

Like two ghosts
in history
we stand together.
Listen to echoes
stir the breeze
and in remembering
take comfort.

I Never Knew

Purple blackness floats
Soft. Low. Wind and memories
Whisper through the leaves

I take your hand, clouds roll away and you are holding mine.

Side by side we walk through streets awash with silhouettes, tree-branch fingers ready to whisk us away. Your warm hand, soft voice gives comfort. We have left our home but I know we are somehow safe.

The sun still shines though day ebbs away. Your hand holds mine as you lead the way to boarding school, let go only when it's time to say goodbye.

You walk with me through the Gardens to my first music exam, name the roses, the lilies not yet in bloom. You note major points, take my hand, assure me I play well.

So many times you guided my way, but knew when to set me free.

My wedding day, you clasp both my hands, tell me you love me, wish me a life full of happiness.

Today, your hand in mine, you look so small, almost childlike as I hum the old-time songs you love to hear.

Soft winds cradle you
Birds no longer sing

I never knew, until now, how hard it was to let go.

Illusive Shadow

A whisper on the wind, a memory
wing of a butterfly pinned forever
in intensity and charm.
    I saw you yesterday
    hair flicked over your shoulder -
    You smiled, I smiled back.
    Last week I caught a glimpse of you
    Your walk, the shape of your head.
You have left us
But I see your face in every crowd.
    Today the ripple of your laughter,
    lifted on the wind
    filled the empty spaces.

In Memoriam

Behind glass, edged with silver
the photo of a young woman
unfaded by years.
Untouched smile
Blue- grey eyes
gentle features
loved and familiar
so close
hands again curl my hair
with rags torn from old sheets,
tuck me in at night
as you read tales of Pollyanna
Still I cannot be glad

In Memory of a Friend

I kneel in chapel
white-washed faces
Pagliacci smiles
voices
void of reason

Stop all the clocks Auden wrote
I understand now,
need
the world to stand,
as the heart, all time – still

You taught me
to cherish
a touch -
gave friendship meaning,
lit dark spaces

Pale walls close in
aisles empty of life
I trace the line of your
rose-wood coffin
glance at stained glass panels
see brightness
remember
       'If I can, I'll send a sign.'
       I bathe in the peace
       sing the last amen.

In the Rhythm of Rain

You watched water
flow down glass -
traced with your finger
sang - *'Listen to the rhythm*
of the falling rain'
You were young
but the words
rang true

        I never understood,
        only knew -
        trees bowed their heads,
        clouds cried -
        daffodils
        failed to bloom.

You tended
roses, violets
fed the doves -
for a while
you sang sweetly,
smiled.

        Now I watch water
        flow down glass,
        hum softly -
        the rhythm of rain
        and remember.

Interlude

The Spirit of Night
waits
for Darkness
to smooth out twilight
so she may
flirt among shadows
dance and twist
into a thousand shapes
away from burning eyes
until
first light
dissolves her essence
and one senses
a lover's
bitter sweet
departure.

In the Stillness

Mt Ainslie –
War Memorial
close now, but still too far away.
Every time I read one of the post cards
From Somewhere in France, the feeling grew.
The ink fades but you become more real.
The knowing of you grand-dad
comes from between the lines.
I need to place a scarlet poppy
  on the honour roll,
  next to your name.

One foot on the bottom step - main entrance
  commemorative pool, eternal flame
  my heart beats faster.
Above white walls,
arches frame the Roll of Honour.
I place the poppy, take photos,
  finger your name, fight back tears.
  In the stillness I recall your words.

September 19th, 1917.
> *'I know you must be lonely,*
> *I can tell you I am*
> *and will be glad*
> *when I can get home with you again.*
> *Now Dear I will close, our big day is tomorrow.*
> *Love to all …. kisses for dear little Edie and Dulcie*
> *not forgetting your Dear self.*
> *I am always your own loving hubby William.*

You express pleasure, relief almost,
 at receiving three letters from your beloved
before going into battle
mention having written
a long letter the day before.
Did you know somehow…

> A soldier pipes the last post
> I stand tall –
> Regret we never met.

Inner Child

I remember a sky full of promise
the moon as a friend
stars that shared secret dreams
a white cold breath – shadows

Death of hope – trust
magic of youth, salad days - passed
no sparkle in blue-grey eyes
staring back from the mirror

What was this enchantment
freedom of inner spirit
to sing with birds
laugh with babbling brooks

Tasting the winds of other worlds
beautiful things full of colour
Ordering up rainbows, moon-beams
questions without answers.

>It's in the heart
>blessed window of loveliness
>fire and passion, but innocence
>makes it precious

Last Call

They say you are tall
Federici
of striking appearance
grey at temples
immaculate in evening dress
You died opening night
as final curtain fell
Saturday March third
eighteen eighty eight
'in a strangely tragic manner'
You haunt, late at night
Melbourne's Princess Theatre
brush past in passageways
sit dress-circle, second row centre
watch the stage.
> Do you hunger for applause
> the footlights
> smell of grease paint
> or consider selling your soul
> to sing again Faust's final aria
> recapture the past
> success bound to follow?

Legacy of Love

Mother's empty room
Lilies of the valley, roses
Grandma's china cabinet full
of memories, white china basket
adorned with red roses, blue
forget-me-nots – *'Think of me'*
written in gold

>*Military Camp Dec 1916*
>*Dear sweetheart*
>*Leaving tonight for France.*
>*Now don't worry dear*
>*we may not get into the firing line*
>*for some time. Be happy*
>*and take care of yourself*
>>*Tons of love to the two little ones*
>>*Not forgetting your dear self*
>>*I am always your own loving husband*

Figurine 'Child in prayer'
A gift at my mother's birth.
    His medals.

>*Fritz has sent shells over*
>*knocked a few villages about but we're safe*
>*Three days to Xmas. It will be so lonely here.*
>*Hope you and the little ones*
>*have a happy one*

Postcards

Purple and yellow pansies, Irises
fronting a moonlit lake
Bunch of red roses

> *A thousand kisses from a loving heart*

More cards from somewhere in France
Charleroi – Rue de la Montagne – Le Deversoir
Renescure – A Place - Eglise

> *A few places visited when camped nearby.*
> *We used to go to this Church every Sunday.*

Satin stitched flowers – '*Yours aye*'
A young soldier kissing his girl

> *A few lines as it's New Years night.*
> *Would love to be with you*
> *and the dear little ones but I am about*
> *fourteen thousand miles away.*
> *I hope and trust I will be home next*
> *New Year*

One *Happy Birthday* postcard stands alone.

*I'm sending a birthday postcard
to dear little Dulcie. Wish I could send
something better. Never mind I will be home
for her fourth birthday, I hope, and will give her
something nice.*

The black-edged telegram sits a little to the left.

Liquid Shadows

Sunlight
winks at the undergrowth
dances with shadows
seeks enchantment
God's masterpiece

Damp earth, aged wood
gossamer webs bejewelled
as dawn's misty curtain
scrolls back, unveils
canopies of ancient forests
silent spectators
to sacred rights

Finds trees of green and gold
lending fragrant breath
shade in which to dream
and a far faint trace
of lost antiquity

Living Drums
Villanelle

Attend the rhythm, low resounding thrum
the raw exotic sounds of jungle lore,
the call to life in living heart of drum.

Be one with earth, slip off your shoes, become
the child within, be free to dance once more.
Attend the rhythm, low resounding thrum

the message echoing untamed, succumb
to passion's frenzy, beat of drum. Explore
the call to life in living heart of drum

it's mighty pulse, ignite your fire and come
with burning ardour to the flame, the core.
Attend the rhythm, low resounding thrum

the ancient laws, the songs our fathers hum
to heal, transport old souls, to bless, restore
the call to life in living heart of drum

a call of wild, that lies so deep, the sum
of all we were before we closed the door.
Attend the rhythm, low resounding thrum
the call to life in living heart of drum.

Made to Measure

Seconds pass before I know
what I'm looking at.
Images flood, the weekend before
my first Saturday-hop.

Mum's inside creating a rope petticoat,
she'd already made a flared skirt.
Dad's in the shed delving into a box -
places templates on black suede,
outlines, cuts each piece.
I want to ask – instead assess every move

He positions a *'Last'* on the bench - my size!
I must be fidgeting because dad smiles,
"Be patient you'll know soon enough."
moulds the front upper – stretches, pulls.
"Get the iron will you."
I didn't recognise it at first, almond shaped,
bigger of course but not like Mum's.
"It shrinks the leather. Draws it into curves."

He threads a leather-work needle,
rummages through his box again -
"Looking for bee's wax."
I think he's telling me to mind my own business.
"Go ask your mum for a candle"
 I don't understand until he runs it along the hemp.
"Makes it easier to use."

A boot! He's making me desert boots.
"and I've bought electric pink shoelaces."
 How lucky was I then, how lucky now
to discover dad had kept my boots.
I hug them to my chest,
take in the faint smell of leather,
thank him for them   and
for the memory.

Magic Of The Night

Vermilion threads weave
gold across blue, stitch
day into night
West wind stirs the leaves
wheat fields rustle talk and
I listen to the gum trees creak
speak aloud the stories
needing to be told
As moon-light shadow-dances
its light silvers the lake   and
I begin to understand

May Day
for Australia

It is said
The fair maid who, the first of May,
Goes to the fields at break of day,
and washes in dew from the hawthorn tree,
will ever after handsome be.
This not-so-fair maid wishes to know
if she buys a hawthorn tree, will it grow
and if it grows, is it the tree
that is to set her beauty free
the time of day
the month of May
or does the magic come with Spring -
if so, should she do the right thing
and always remember
the first of September
to wash in dew from her Hawthorn tree
so forever handsome she will be.

Moonspell

Pale moon, a sphere of silver mercury
against soft velvet night to help us heal.
You are, with brother sun, the unity -
intuitive, all spiritual ideal
we seek. Alone, the blushing bride of gold,
young Artemis and Nature's growing guide.
A sister to Apollo, strong and bold,
you stand apart, control the evening tide.
To us, chameleon, a whispered sigh
 a ruse believed when structured like a smile.
You're Alpha to Omega, eagle high,
our lion, dragon, raven, silver mile.
In dreams, become the essence of white-light,
self knowledge, ceaseless wisdom, pure delight

Nightmares

Unknown icons in the dark
A strange hieroglyphic mark
Shadows prowl across the wall
Demon voices shriek and call
Mock our pathos as they pass
Secluded spaces
Alien faces
Cats eyes strobe strong and bright
Phantoms wander through the night
    Pursued by footsteps loud and clear
    Run the gauntlet of our fear
    Loose the bond of a winding sheet
    Leave the nightmare incomplete

On Mount Parnassus

ancestral voices awaken within
whisper of pages unwritten
a generation of women
heard the music
but never danced.
      Halcyon wings
      stir waters of Castalia
      carry Terpsichore's gifts.
           I drink from the fountain
           step onto the proscenium
           lift purple petticoats
           dance.

Overture to Night

Day fades -   street lights flicker
a thousand crickets
tune perfect pitch
and a curtain opens to night.
Winds blow softly, cars whirr past
add low tones
variations to the music
the clink of dishes silver triangles
for percussion
a mopoke calls her mate
and the symphony begins.

Paint the Wind

Paint the wind so I may see
The wind that colours my destiny

The wind that spreads the colours bold
Across the sky and times of old
The golden streaks of sunset's glow
The purple blackness soft and low

The wind that moves like shadows grey
The clustered clouds of night away
The misty blanket of the morn
All signs of night before the dawn

The wind that plays with every tree
That quickens and stirs the living sea
Like silver ripples through the grass
To toss and swirl and gently pass

A scented heat, a warning light
A black and swollen stormy night
A thunderbolt upon a hill
Then holds its breath and all is still

So paint the wind that I may see
The wind that colours my destiny

Painted Devils

Long stealing shadows
painting devils
on the bedroom wall.
Angry voices,
that come as a dream.

Doors moan.
Footsteps echo.
The game begins

> *Where are we going Mummy?*
> *Is Daddy coming?*
>   *Hush Darling.*

Hand in hand
once more we travel darkened streets
to the one who'll take us in.

The make-shift bed never remembered.
Nor the journey home.

Only long stealing shadows
and painted devils.

Paradise

Beyond the dream
through clouds
a glimpse, a vision
Heaven sent

No Elysium fields,
 wind blown grasslands,
tall Oaks, Karris or Gums
under which to rest awhile –
no vanilla rosettes of honeysuckle.

A resurfacing into light
from a great depth -
a warm glow within
a stillness, a knowing
this is…

Portals

Aged, stripped bare
you stand proud and firm
one-time main-stay
portal to her life
Watched as they carried her in
Supported her father
heavy and tired from work
Remember, with pride
a day the gate swung wide
her first sulky ride to town
Later
she brought her own children.
You felt the aging in you limbs
as they swung back and forth
squealed with delight
grew up
left.
Silence stretched.
Her tears made patterns in the dust
the mail box empty.
Now she passes
one last time
through your gate
The gate her father built
to keep her in.

Portrait of a Tree

Burnt, charred
dressed in mourning
black and grey,
your branches
rise in prayer -
touch my heart
my soul
Through tears
see again your
browns and greens
blush of red -
sunlight dancing
on your leaves
wind scurry from
brother to sister
father, friend
Now in majesty, true dignity
stripped bare,
you stand proud, splendid
in you symmetry
witness to Creation's truth
death is not the end.

Recall

Each inebriated blow
punctuates her screams
bruises her self worth
she cowers
back to the wall
steels herself
against the pleas
the promises
        One day she will leave.

Rhubarb and Plums

The women of the neighbourhood
claimed him as their own
He gave time
which belonged to his wife.
Bestowed gifts, fresh fish
filleted, of course
home grown rhubarb and plums

He had a daughter, wanted a son
one to take fishing.
At six, she sawed pieces of wood
fashioned a footstool   but
used the precious copper-heads
needed for his boat.

At thirteen, helped restore an old hull
moulded planks over fire and steam.
He never gave thanks
Knew at last
she'd never please him.

    His daughter waited - watched
    and learned.

Now part of the school choir
With strengths of her own
she challenged him with a song
They sang, hit the high notes
held, sustained.
She won.

She was pretty, they said
had his talent, his voice -
a lucky man.
In front of neighbours
she charmed
extra pocket money,
late curfews.

    At eighteen,
     with a man of her own
    she finally gained his attention
    Too late.

Riding the Wind

A midnight stallion races untamed wind.
An eagle hovers, shrills its haunting cry,
awakening my soul to dreams still pinned
to flights of fantasy, the child too shy,
afraid - to free the power deep inside,
of secrets held in darkness, brutal light,
to dance beneath the moon or choose to ride
with stars, believe in magic, know the night.
But now I race fey wind along the shore
and soar past golden eagles to disperse
soft clouds, frolic and flirt with mighty Thor
until his passion fills my universe,
my senses, firing life's true destiny
to ride wild horses, fly as eagles - free

Sanctuary
My Hearts Crystal Cave

Wrapped in Pete's dressing gown, I drift through rooms. Nothing has changed but I find it difficult sometimes to visualise Pete in these rooms, yet he's all around me.

I curl into his chair, hug his book trying to understand, when I hear tapping at my door.

Through the screen I face a raven, a crystal on a cord around his neck.

Had he been playing with a neighbour's sun-catcher?

When Pete fed the birds he'd laugh, say if he could come back it would be as a bird.

I step onto the patio and the bird hops back, tilts his head.

I watch my unexpected guest circle, strut to the lawn and with short head movements indicate a dying fern, a stunted palm.

Tangled roots twist,
Turn relentless in their struggle
cling to life

I wish Pete had held to life. I was angry, yelled at him for giving up, not trying. Realised later he'd found inner peace.

I turn away. The raven's beside me pacing. I know from Pete and the way he talked to the birds, I must follow.

The raven's silver eyes hold me and I feel like a child being chastised.

The Crystal, a piece of mischief maybe, should have told me.

The very book that meant so much, about Merlin and the boy Arthur, in the crystal cave. Pete had tried to explain the crystal cave as a privileged place inside the human heart. I didn't understand, but bend to rip dead stalks from ferns and golden cane, weed blades of grass creeping in from the lawn, discover a purple blossom hidden under a wide leaf, sit back and look to my new found friend. He has gone.

Shades of evening colour what is left of day as I turn, walk inside and lock the door.

Alone, I can't resist a glimpse through the verticals.

Silhouettes, shadows
along pathways he trod
flowers he grew

Fantasies of light and shadow beat distant drums, invite me to celebrate the mysteries that can only be experienced in darkness. I refuse the invitation, retreat to my room and drift into a land of nightmares.

Soft morning sunlight filters through the drapes. I reach for Pete's dressing gown and recall the oasis he created with ferns and palms. Look towards his photo and promise never to neglect it again. It's then I remember the rose garden he planted for me.

Perfume of roses
wafts silently across time
stirs the memory

I struggle with images of my husband and myself laughing, planning the garden around our retirement cottage. When I said I wanted roses he confessed he loved them but was sure they didn't like him. He never went near them without being scratched but always cared for them. And I...

The raven's eyes catch my attention. I run from the room and stand in the middle of the lawn.

He flies across the gate. I follow. I see the roses, their large dried heads void of perfume and colour. With tears rolling down my cheeks I cut away the spent flowers, water-distorted buds struggling to blossom.

Like my friend's feathers they sparkle with promise.

"Thank you" It seems right but I'm not sure why until he flies high, circles, then settles in a gum tree. The leaves are dark, almost black against the sun

Nightfall finds me alone until moonlight illuminates my gum tree and a small flicker of light reflects from among its leaves.

My hearts crystal cave
a haven, a sacred place
dwells inside me.

Scarred

She serves homage
on silver lined plates
fixes a smile
at business lunches
watches him select
delectable
little number
for dessert
sits
waits out mind games
constrains tears
threatening to spill
      Steaming waters
      simmer too long
      boil dry
      leave
      blackened shell

Sea Sprite

In aqua pool adorned in lacy white
she dives, shy ocean spirit, anxious bride
awaiting winter waves to show their might

to raise her up, take wing on freedom's flight
towards a deeper blue, no more to hide
in aqua pool adorned in lacy white.

Her only solace, dark and secret night
who never understood her lack of pride
awaiting winter waves to show their might,

to boldly lift her veil, caress, unite,
become as one and never more reside
in aqua pool adorned in lacy white

until a golden moon whispers his delight,
reveres her beauty, charm, at ebb of tide
awaiting winter waves to show their might.

Her smile reflects his praise, then shining bright
she radiates, content for life inside
an aqua pool adorned in lacy white
no longer waiting waves to show their might.

Sestina of a Letter Home - 1917

I write to you from war-torn France, dear Dad
assure both you and Mum that I am safe.
So few remain; the wounded shipped back home,
the fallen left to help wild flowers grow.
We hear the shells exploding night and day,
and disillusioned men, who fight for peace,

their freedom, country, pray this hour for peace
to not relive the horror, pain. Dear Dad
I pray this war ends soon, await the day
our brave Australians are once more safe,
released from fear and sadness, free to grow
beside their sweethearts, loved ones left at home

Here only old folk stay, defend their home.
I'm sure this land is beautiful in peace
when fields, unfenced, turn green as grasses grow
with spring and trees bear fruit. But sadly Dad
delays our Aussie troops at least a day
the Germans torch those trees. It keeps them safe,

These people labour long and hard each day,
to cultivate the soil, protect their home
and farmlands knowing they are far from safe
Equipment here is out of date, so peace
won't bring relief from heavy toil, but Dad
these folk resist, earn our respect and grow.

My girls improve of late, I'm told they grow
in health and strength, more beautiful each day
since leaving Albany. I ask you Dad
and Mum to visit soon my wife and home.
Please tell me all is well, it gives me peace
to hear my Jane, my little girls, are safe

I end this now and trust that you are safe,
Ask Mum to write me how her roses grow
at summer's end. Her letters bring me peace,
as do my Jane's. They give me hope the day
will come when families will live at home
as one. For now my darling Mum and Dad,

I wish for peace, my dear ones to be safe
and pray, dear Dad, as scarlet poppies grow
I will return one day to heart and home
.

Setting The Stage

Old musicals resonate
from violin strings
drift into a fanfare of
magic and memories
My daughter listens to
hits of the eighties
recalls her first dance
rock concert
wedding day
I spin melodies
to my grandson
The Lion King
Pocahontas
and Aladdin
pray one day they
remind him of me

Smouldering Embers

Music books spill
from the old suitcase
The Pianist's Mentor,
The Concise Oxford Dictionary of…
The Listener's History of…
manuscripts - theory, composition
biographies - Chopin, Grieg,
Verdi, Mozart,
and my favourite –
whose bust sits atop
the piano mother left me.

Beethoven's music rippled
through my childhood -
hours listening to mother play,
frustration as my small fingers
struggled with chords.
The orchestra -
my first -
rush of awareness
riding every scale, chord.
Tragedy, strength, fire
detonate in kaleidoscopic colour
diffuse into sated hues of molten embers
never dying.

Beethoven's Fifth explodes
I hear again
sweet flutes, richer clarinets

strings, highs – lows.
every note consuming.
Violoncello, double - bass
dancing through the Scherzo.
Kettledrum's tap,
above violin's soft melody.
Piccolo pianissimo,
trombones triumphant,
each clear
above the storm.
My heart,
all instruments, crescendo,
awaken
        forgotten passions
        Mother's gift.

Soft Voice, Rich and Clear

Giant poplars,
Silent sentries, unbending to my
humble petition

Outside the cathedral doors I wait, ready to begin my new life. A summer breeze riffles dry leaves, lifts my veil and I see again that small girl holding her mother's hand, walk through these same grounds, cross the road.

A warm kiss and my mother's hand slips away as a large iron gate closes behind me. I face a convent built of lime-stone blocks, a hundred years old, like the church where I was christened wearing a white crochet gown embroidered with pink french-knot roses, all stitched by Nan - which now lies in my treasure chest in my new home.

I turn towards the boarding school, try to understand the cement wasteland I see under my feet as I pass a small convent chapel. Hope, rays of a fading sun caught in the lilies on its stained glass window and the avenue of shady trees coming into view.

I stay awhile, stare at the Gums, white giants, breathe in the scent of eucalyptus, and smell the freshly mown lawn.

Nan's rose filled garden
Daisy meadows, soft warm lambs
preludes to freedom

Then I see it, the sign - do not walk on the grass.

I close my eyes to dreams, face a summer of concrete steps.

Other children now, big and little, gather on an old wooden verandah which tugs again at memories, time spent with Nan.

My eyes lock in a watery daydream as I follow a line of girls, watch boards bend under my feet, see a rickety stairway, appearing to go forever upwards towards heaven. Nan went to heaven.

> beyond the sunset
> blue hills above the river
> resting in the clouds

My knees weaken. The steps leading to the little girl's dormitory, so high, so dark. Then I see a halo of light, which somehow guides me to the top.

The perfume of roses drifts through candlelight in front of a painting. Two small children stand halfway across a bridge fording a fast running stream. Behind and above these two little ones spreads the wings of their guardian angel and for the first time I smile.

When my parents parted Gran became my refuge.

> Rain splattered window
> tears, angry words, a parting
> Lonely ride to Nan's

I know she still protects me as I walk to the window near my bed, listen to unfamiliar sounds of a busy street at night and yawn.

Staying a moment longer I stare across the river to distant hills, leave my fears among the stars and wink at the moon

> brighter at day's end

a yellow path to meet me
light dark still waters.

A breeze brushes my cheek as I stand at the cathedral door look to the man waiting for me at the front of the church.
Grandma guided my steps into boarding school, guides me now as I walk down the aisle towards the one I love.

Gentle light above
soft voice, rich and clear
carries on the wind.

Somewhere in France

> War clouds rumble black
> purgatorial shadows
> unknown shores ahead.

I read postcards arranged on a table before me, walk in your footsteps.

I am somewhere in France, stand beside you for long wet hours, awaiting inspection. I shiver, wipe away tears for you, for the loved ones you had to leave behind.

Nervously, I march in your footprints through ice and mud-filled shell holes. Follow your battalion through Buire, Fricourt, Mametz to Waterlot Farm. You never mention the battles fought, the lives lost but your postcards invite me to see you dig ditches, watch how the people continue to work their land though their homes have been shelled, their crop, fruit trees, cut down, burned.

I am beginning to understand the need to carry on, to believe all is not lost.

You long to be with your wife and two small girls. You tell her not to worry but I am sensing a longing to share, say more than '*I am well*' as I crouch by your side in muddy dark ditches.

Black twisted trees are marring the landscape, hiding the sky. I shudder, know now your need for more letters is a plea for hope, a walk in sunshine.

I promise to write to my own girls more often.

Terrified, I picture encounters to come, bayonet battles, thick woods.

> trees you planted grow well
> their sun-kissed leaves dancing
> among the shadows.

Silhouettes, truths I do not search out, images I block.

In tears I turn to the postcard of a church in Renescure, hear the echoes of prayers offered at its altar, miles from loved ones, hoping, trusting they are safe, that you will be home next year.

I follow one battle to the next, aware the distant guns sounding night and day, wanting to learn but afraid.

The thought - mine or yours - of dying, being alone.

For the first time you mention a battle, the wounded being sent to England, a few to Australia.

'The rest help the wildflowers grow.'

> scarlet poppies
> look toward blue skies -
> hope marches on.

You rest and I breathe deeply, take in your wonder at the changes around you -

the fine shady trees, the strawberries, red currents popping up here and there, the long grass covering shell holes and the transport horses feeding on self-growing crop.

I know you will be in the thick of it again soon but for now you are safe and I smile at your words playing before me - the organised football matches, laughter, talk of families, loved ones, the smell of gum tips burning.

Summertime, a push to The Somme, a victory of sorts.

I struggle with news to come, end my journey where you, grandfather, found joy in the song of a Lark, renewed strength from countryside in spring.

I learn hope is sometimes all we have. All we need.

        a Golden Wattle
grows alongside the road home -
      my yellow ribbon.

Song of Twilight

The day remains in dying streaks of gold
until fey Twilight spreads her cloak of grey
and waits for purple blackness, dark and bold,
to smooth the eventide, all trace of day,
permitting her to flirt with clouds, to twist
and dance a thousand miles from starlit skies
fragmented light behind soft velvet mist
enfold with Darkness who demands no guise.
Now through the dusky hours of dimmest night
they rouse the wind and softly breezes croon
caress the shadows, spinning pure delight
as they embrace above an ebbing moon.

As day's new light dissolves the magic spell
we taste a lover's bitter-sweet farewell

Tabula Rasa

Without a night from which
troubles can be soothed -
without the promise
each new day brings
are we
mother's milk
seeds sown in silt
that little black dress
rage-red sweater
or
a virginal christening gown
and for the moment
tabula rasa

        Old memory stirs
        wild flesh, moods, ideas
        languages of
        poetry and passion
        shower of sparks
        stable of coloured horses
        letting live, letting die

Through the Darkness

Melancholy
cries through you–
rides on a memory
wraiths of pale fog
larceny of hope
self-worth
stumbling in shadows
alone, afraid
until
from the gloaming of hell,
comes a glow

>Through darkness,
>burns the yellow sun

Through the Mist

Ideas, creativity and life
thrive on underground rivers,
little freshers
pouring into our lives

Lashings
find their mark
permeate the soul
steal self-esteem
suffocate

Crippled spectre
of former selves
we wander confused
through a haze

> What is that cry
> over the sea,
> voice on the wind?
>
> An Old One
> Calling
> until something within
> responds

To the Tree
Outside my Window

You wave a friendly greeting through the glass
I smile to see you dance a minuet
politely bowing every time I pass.
I now admire your leaves all shining wet
in morning's early dew, and hear your song
an old familiar tune, an ardent prayer
upon the wind, to call the ancient one
remind him that we share one soul, we care.
I've loved you since I planted you so long
ago, have watched you grow both tall and strong
to spread your arms and shade me from the sun.

To Your Dear Self

To my dear little ones, your own sweet self.
All missing letters, long awaited news
arrived today. I feared they would remain
forever lost aboard the sunken ship
off Freo. Pleased to hear you're safe and sound
to know, so far, you have not gone without

too much. It's hard to carry on without
the thought of you at home, for by myself
I'm incomplete. The cold and constant sound
of guns has made me long for all your news.
 I worry, ever since that first war ship
set sail, that only memories remain.

Please know dear one, my love and thoughts remain
with you, our precious little girls. Without
you by my side, I curse each battle ship
that carries me away from your dear self
to foreign lands. It's only hometown news
that keeps me sane, allows me hear the sound

of your sweet voice, my girls at play, the sound
of laughter. Your calm words help me remain
in touch. The men all crowd the mail for news
from home. Believe me my dear wife, without
those letters from loved ones, there's little self
regard, for some, a reason to jump ship,

To risk their lives, secure an early ship
back home; for sadly, some strong men, once sound
of mind, are now confused, no use to self,
their men, their mates. If trust does not remain
steadfast, not many will survive. Without
knowledge Australia is safe, your news,

I'd die inside, so please keep sending news
and know I thank the Lord for every ship,
that carries mail from dearest ones. Without
something to cling to, that uncommon sound
of mail-call merriment, what would remain
of reason. Pray, please stay your own sweet self.

Without your love, your treasured, longed for news,
the knowledge your dear self awaits my ship,
only the sound of dying would remain.

Trust

As children
we questioned
Now we search –
an elusive soul mate
eternal youth
the Holy Grail
peace and love
of this world
while
underground rivers -
nurture earth
the roots of trees
and a mother offers
her babe a breast.

Twilight of the Gods

Greed consumed
the Gods of Asgard
civilisation vanished, left
naked earth - until
a new sun
another generation of gods
faded the enchantment
of mythical forests

Prayers forsaken
we rushed into the sun
craved gold and gems
forgot
the promise of a rainbow
wisdom gleaned
through ancient writings

Garnet, turquoise
saffron blended
became mud -
rainforests dwindled
lakes desiccated
our land
exposed

Chaos reigns
clouds edged with guilt
bask in a misted moon
prophets wail warnings.

Undiminished Symphony

Footsteps echo along the hallway,
trinkets breathe for space
in satin lined boxes,
cushions and pillows
cling to old impressions.

If you stand
outside the lounge-room door
Fleur- de –lis, Rustle of Spring
Riffle through an old iron frame
Edge into the room
and the melodies float away.

Shy even now.

But that same timid smile,
reflected in photos
steals across the faces
of her grandchildren
traces a return
to where bedtime stories,
music and laughter
lit the darkness

Watching Snails

Chloe giggles.
Her delight
a snail's silver trace across the lawn
path to adventure
a moment of happiness.

    I spent years
    searching through clouds
    to find a patch of blue
    the promised lining.

I watch Chloe discover
dew-drops on gossamer webs
fairy- wings caught in morning sun-
see magic
between light and shadow
the sparkle in my daughter's eyes
silver at my feet.

When rain mists the blue

Purple blackness floats
wind and memories
whisper through the leaves
I take your hand
clouds roll away.

      We walk through streets
      awash with silhouettes
      your warm hand
      comforts me
      you lead the way
      let go
      only when it's time
      to say goodbye.

      My first music exam.
      We walk through gardens
      you name roses
      lilies not yet in bloom -
      assure me
      I play well.

      My wedding day.
      You clasp my hands
      tell me you love me
      wish me happiness

Your hand in mine,
your face small, childlike.
Soft winds cradle you
 rain mists the blue
birds no longer sing.

Why?

The dog kennel sits complete
awaits a coat of paint, its maker's return.
He will never come and I
have not the heart to relinquish
my husband's work.

The grandchildren
have been told not to ask.
Why do I hesitate -
Because he won't be here
to share, see their smiling faces?
I complained
said it took too much
of his time.

I remember the way he smiled,
shaped, shaved and hammered.
He loved the stupid thing, wanted
so much to finish it.

> I look towards the clock,
> phone my daughter,
> ask her to drop in
> with the children
> after school -
> to bring old clothes
> be prepare to paint.

Writer on the Bus

Colonial cream, Mission brown
Federation Green
re-wind past the window.
Lights turn red.

She scribbles across the page
An idea almost understood
fast passes with every car.

Another stop
A Commodore below.
Mobile phone
Call to the wife?
Negotiating a deal?
or
cappuccino for two
in some quiet cubicle
Her pen races with meatier stuff.
She can hear the smile in his voice.
Breakfast before work?
He could get away for lunch.
The lights turn green

Yesterday and Today

I love you
when you disobey my rules
are polite to my friends
give that cheeky grin

But don't tell me you're gay
I wouldn't know what to say

I loved you when
you were born
were never troubled
by sleepless nights -
when you cried
your first day at school

But don't tell me you're gay
I wouldn't know what to say

I loved you when
eager for your first school dance
you stood, uneasy in a dress –
And yes, when you
clipped your curls
wore your hair black and spiked
I love the way
you're looking at me now

tell me — but remember
I may not know what to say
know only — I loved you
through all your yesterdays
and I love you still today

www.ingramcontent.com/pod-product-compliance
Lightning Source LLC
Chambersburg PA
CBHW071529080526
44588CB00011B/1605